DENMARK

I0098059

SERPENT CLUB PRESS
established 2013

Autumn, Again; Spring, Anew
Michael Skelton & Stephen Morel

Circumambulate
Daniel Bossert

Moon on Water
Matthew Gasda

New Writing: Volume I

New Writing: Volume II

On Bicycling: An Introduction
Samuel Atticus Steffen

Sonata for Piano and Violin
Matthew Gasda

The Substitute
Michael Skelton

FORTHCOMING...

A Quarter Century
Eda

DENMARK

A play by Matthew Gasda

Serpent Club Press

DENMARK
Copyright © Serpent Club Press, 2016
All rights reserved

Serpent Club Press books may be purchased for educational, business, or sales
promotional use. For more information please contact Serpent Club Press at
theserpentclub@gmail.com

First Edition

Printed in the United States of America
Set in Williams Caslon
Designed by Emily Gasda

ISBN
9780997613407

LCCN
2016908221

DENMARK

A play in three acts

by Matthew Gasda

DENMARK had its world premiere at The Gallery Space at The Access Theater in New York City, opening on June 2, 2016 (Kim Sweet, Producer). It was directed by Vanessa Koppel; the set design was by Tate Rekhlau and Jacqueline Brockel; the costume design was by Benjamin Stevenson; both set and costumes design were overseen by Deb O; lighting design was by Michael Blagys; the dramaturg was Daniel Bossert; the stage manager was Jillian Christensen. The cast was as follows:

HARPER . . . . Adriene Moreno

MASON . . . . Jonathan Wilde

ELAINE . . . . Katherine Wessling

PAUL . . . . Brian McCormack

RYAN . . . . PJ Adzima

CHARACTERS

HARPER College student. 22

MASON English teacher in NYC private school. 40

PAUL Father of HARPER and RYAN. Philosophy professor in NYC. 58

ELAINE Mother of HARPER and RYAN. A former artist. 52

RYANHarper's twin, college student. 22

Apparent race: open.

SETTING

Winter. Morning.

The action takes place at the family's beach house within driving distance of NYC.

The stage is divided between living area with couches and chairs and small kitchenette. The front door of the stage is located along the back center of the stage. On either side of the door are windows, which look out on dunes, and further in the distance, on the sea. (The house is clearly located on the beach).

To the left and right of the stage are doors which presumably lead to bed and bathrooms.

ACT I

The stage is dark.

Door shuts off-stage.

Cue sound of shower turning on.

Shower stops.

Enter HARPER from stage-left (with wet hair, and cup of coffee in her hand), who turns on a lamp.

Enter MASON, his hair also wet.

HARPER

You aim your depression like a gun—

MASON

Bang bang.

HARPER

Make eye-contact with me—

MASON

No.

HARPER

Mason, I want to have sex again.

MASON

Not right now.

HARPER
I'm going to scream—

MASON
Ok.

MASON sits down at the coffee-table and turns on a second light. MASON rolls up a magazine from the coffee-table and hands it to HARPER.

HARPER screams through the rolled up magazine and then puts it back town.

MASON
Do you feel better?

HARPER
No.

MASON
Here—

MASON hands HARPER the magazine; HARPER rolls it up again, puts it her mouth again as if to scream. She takes a deep breathe, and puts the magazine down again, not having screamed.

HARPER
You get away with things that nobody else does with me, I let you in—and I don't let anybody in…I don't think there's anyone else to let in… and if there was somebody else in my life, I would probably check to see if it was you in disguise.

MASON

Don't you ever question that feeling Harper?

HARPER

Yes.

MASON

And—

HARPER

I'm not an idiot.

MASON

I didn't say you were.

HARPER

Then don't ask me condescending questions.

MASON

Ok.

HARPER

Is it bad that you're the only person who makes
me happy?

MASON

You don't know what makes you happy.

HARPER

Come over here—

MASON

I'm too busy resurfacing for air to touch you
right now.

HARPER

You've had plenty of time to catch your breath—

MASON

And you've had plenty of time to calm down.

HARPER

I don't know what to fucking do with you
sometimes! You're such a incredible turd. React to
something! Please—

MASON

Reaction is counterproductive.

HARPER

I'm trying to be close to you—

MASON

I just can't convey my emotions directly; I'm sorry.

HARPER

The first time I talked to you, like really talked to
you, you said that innocence was the only thing
that really interested you—in people…and I've
never, ever forgotten that you said that. And I
couldn't forget it: because it was a warning.

MASON

What kind of warning?

HARPER

That you'd stop loving me if I stopped being
innocent—

MASON

Perhaps.

HARPER

And I've stopped being innocent—

MASON

Anyway who says that is still innocent.

HARPER

Then why have you stopped loving me?

MASON

I don't know.

HARPER

You're like a radiator, except the room only gets colder and colder.

MASON

Put on a sweater then.

Exit HARPER, upset.

MASON

(directed off-stage)

Kafka once said: 'there is infinite hope except for us.'

Enter HARPER in an extra-large sweater.

HARPER

I don't want riddles: I want physical affection.

MASON
  And I want physical riddles.

HARPER
  I told someone about us.

MASON
  Harper, that wasn't the best idea...

HARPER
  Mason, don't look so worried; I'm fucking with
  you—I haven't told anyone.

MASON
  Alright.

HARPER
  I like secrets as much as you do.

MASON
  Except I don't like secrets.

HARPER
  What do you like then?

MASON
  The mathematics of light—

HARPER
  You just say these things...that are impossible to
  respond to.

MASON
  But you always have a response—

HARPER

You expect me to be something I'm not, clearly.

MASON

Which is what?

HARPER

Pure of heart.

MASON doesn't respond.

HARPER

I don't like sitting next to someone and not speaking. It makes me feel like a movie's about to begin.

MASON

Maybe a movie is about to begin—

HARPER

But what movie?

MASON

It's a silent picture.

HARPER

Sounds like a movie about us.

MASON lays down on the ground, stares at the ceiling.

MASON

What if we could project our whole relationship right now onto the ceiling—would you lay here with me and watch it?

HARPER
  No.

MASON
  Why not?

HARPER
  Because that would mean it was over.

  MASON sits up.

MASON
  I like love better when it's over.

HARPER
  I like love better when it's beginning.

MASON
  Most people do—

HARPER
  Except for you—

MASON
  I feel like I'm walking on a tight-rope suspended
  between you and nowhere...or, no: like I've
  fallen from the tight-rope and am still falling.

HARPER
  That's not consoling.

MASON
  I'm not trying to be consoling.

HARPER

Maybe you're just upset at how difficult it's been
for you to get it up lately; that would explain a
lot—

MASON

My virtue, my power, my utility: my cock.

HARPER

Am I making you unhappy?

MASON

Still, her body. Never a rose, this flower of
love…My hands, planted within her. My tongue,
curling at her throat.

HARPER

Mason?

MASON

What?

HARPER

What are you doing?

MASON

Letting my words break apart to see if they emit
any light.

HARPER

Oh.

MASON

You should try it—

HARPER

All I require from my words is that they
communicate.

MASON

What a waste of language.

HARPER

Not for me.

MASON

When you were in the school play a few years
ago, you said, 'I think that Chekhov wrote for me
alone. He is the most beautiful man that I can
imagine.'

HARPER

What does that have to do with anything right
now?

MASON

It has to do with your imagining there to be
a special bond where there's just emotional
recklessness and pain—

HARPER

Maybe recklessness and pain are part of our
bond.

MASON

Maybe.

HARPER

  We went to a hotel, the first time—do you
  remember?

MASON

  Vaguely—

HARPER

  I had my eyes open the whole time we were
  fucking, and so did you—

MASON

  Harper—

HARPER

  Does it bother you to hear me talk like this?

MASON

  No.

HARPER

  Then why are you reacting like that?

MASON

  Like I said: the mathematics of light; the flower
  of your hands...

HARPER

  Mason—

MASON

I just want to speak words that make their way
in the world without my emotions attached to
them...but I can't seem to be able to do that
completely; not the way I'd really like to.

HARPER

Why would you possibly want to do that?

MASON

So I could just listen to my words without
hearing myself, like sitting by a stream.

HARPER

I wish I could cut a little square in your skull,
release the pressure—

MASON

There's one mask for tragedy, one mask for
comedy, but there's no mask for the face itself.

HARPER

But I see you Mason—

MASON

Then where I am?

HARPER

Right here—

MASON

Where's here?

HARPER

Next to me, in this quiet moment.

MASON

You understand that I had to meet you, right?
That I had to test myself by meeting you and
letting you love me.

HARPER

Can you just please be direct with me?

MASON

There's no being direct with you Harper; there's
just not—

HARPER

You can't just assert that—

MASON

But I can—

HARPER

I wish you trusted me—

MASON

Trust isn't the issue—

HARPER

I don't let boys talk to me. I pretend I'm
interested, but I'm really thinking about you—

MASON

I can go back to the city early if you want—

HARPER

I'd be unhappy.

MASON

I guess I'll stay for a little while, then. Direction doesn't matter when you're in zero gravity.

HARPER

You're someone who astonishes when they walk in the room. But you're working to undo that part of yourself; and you won't tell me why— and you don't see that I can see it. You think you're such a secret: but really you're not a secret enough—

MASON

The question I always ask myself is: what is the real relationship between the marks on the mathematician's page and the operations out in heaven? I don't understand why the universe behaves in a way that we can predict—

HARPER

It's like you woke up this morning and decided that you wanted me to suffer—

MASON

I'm tired of carrying you from emotion to emotion Harper. My arms have given out.

HARPER

Then put me down: I can walk—

MASON
Only in place—

HARPER
You like having me around to hurt, don't you?

MASON
But you're not hurt.

HARPER
I couldn't be more hurt.

MASON
The sexual orchid blooms—

HARPER
Are you bored of me?—

MASON
And dies—

HARPER
If you're bored of me, please tell me—

MASON
I didn't say I was bored of you.

HARPER
Then let's have sex again—

MASON
The heart wants pause to breathe.

HARPER
Then breathe Mason—

*MASON takes an exaggeratedly deep breath and
exhales loudly.*

HARPER
Do you feel better?

MASON
Well, I'm one breath closer to death.

HARPER
You make me feel happy to be alive.

MASON
Chekhov... Chekhov—why did you think Chekhov
was writing for you and no one else? Because
I think he was writing to pass the time before
tuberculosis consumed him.

HARPER
I have real love inside of me. But you're so
indifferent to it.

MASON
When you speak, Harper, you can sound like your
mother, or me, or your friends and—God knows—
you can even sound like yourself; but—

HARPER
You insist on seeing me as some kind of reckless,
erotic child.

MASON
If the shoe fits—

HARPER

Fucking asshole.

MASON

I don't wake up here the way I wake up in other places, I'm sorry—

HARPER

How do you wake up then?

MASON

Disassociated.

HARPER

From what?

MASON

My speaking voice.

HARPER

Why?

MASON

Because a voice can break free from a person; talks in out of control ways—I'm referring to Shakespeare obviously—

HARPER

Have you noticed how alone you make me feel when you speak to me like this?

MASON

Yes.

HARPER
  Then why don't you stop?

MASON
  I can't.

  HARPER doesn't respond.

MASON
  And you shouldn't want me to stop—

HARPER
  Why?

MASON
  Because this is how I talk in my head.

HARPER
  I have no idea why I thought this weekend was a
  good idea.

MASON
  Because you wanted to fuck as much as you could
  while you had the house—

HARPER
  Shut up.

MASON
  What other reason did you have?

HARPER
  Guess.

MASON

I've already told you my guess.

HARPER

You think that I'm that simple—

MASON

No.

HARPER

You think I'm just a horny teenager—

MASON

No.

HARPER

I don't know how else to interpret what you're saying—

MASON

Then don't interpret at all—

HARPER

Whenever I talk to you, you push my voice into higher and higher registers, so that I always end up feeling shrill and unpleasant—

MASON

I hear a voice that continually halts mid-flight, enchanted by the possibility of looking down.

HARPER

You've never actually fought with me; you've
never actually gotten angry. There's nothing to
you Mason; nothing but evasions—

MASON

Do you know that Botticelli illustrated the entire
Divine Comedy? And that it took about 400
years for Western culture to notice or care? I
mean, we're talking about the greatest poet of
angels being illustrated by the greatest painter of
angels—and no one noticed—I've always found
this completely remarkable—

HARPER

Am I the thing that most excites you in life?

MASON

I don't understand the question—

HARPER

I'm asking if you'd trade me for one of your
favorite poems—

MASON

No one should trade anyone for one of their
favorite poems.

HARPER

That's not what I asked—

MASON

Love is hopeless, so why trade it for a poem?—
which has its own hope—

HARPER

I have no relationship with you, do I?

MASON

You have a relationship to the empty space I
once occupied.

HARPER

I still think you're a miracle. I always will.

MASON

I was just the first mature man to recognize you
as a woman—

HARPER

Is that all it was?

MASON

It's all it still is.

HARPER

You're a coward.

MASON

I'm a realist.

HARPER

Are you kidding?

MASON

Some nights, when you're at my place, I can't
sleep; so I go and sit down in the kitchen, and
take out my legal pad, and I'll write until you
wake up; I'll write and write and write; and
usually—yeah—I'm still crying, off and on;
because of providence, you know? Because of
this sense of providence that shocks me awake;
shocks me out of bed; shocks me into the desire
to make something material out of it. My entire
adult life people have referred to 'my gift'—but
those people don't buy my books, and if they do
they don't read them. But that doesn't matter,
that's not what I'm talking about; that's not what
I care about Harper—I just want them to know
the fury that speaks in me; the fury that keeps
me from speaking; the fury that makes physical
contact with you almost inconceivable...Most
of the time I'm a dead man, I'm nothing; and
then suddenly: I'm too alive; too able to feel
everything; too possessed with the overwhelming
feeling that life is perfect, that life is good,
that people are good and precious and not
to be forgotten...and when people become
precious, then the stakes are changed; then I
feel paralyzed—then I want to go back to that
off-state...when the current isn't flowing...I've
had nothing tragic happen to me...nothing,

nothing...except for what I dream of...what I touch...Because your skin has its own gravity; it warps the framework of the space around it; pulls people in; pulls hands, lips, teeth towards it...

HARPER

Are you ok?

MASON

I'm sorry...

HARPER

For what?

MASON

Setting time in motion.

HARPER

I don't know what to do with you.

MASON

I feel like a satellite fallen out of orbit, a satellite swimming through deep space; a satellite swimming through the place where God used to—

HARPER

I don't want God randomly grafted onto the conversation we're having.

MASON

God is always there—he's always there—He's
the placenta that spills out after the thought's
arrived.

HARPER

What are you talking about? What are we talking
about?

MASON

We're talking about the possibility that I'm
clinically depressed.

HARPER

Are you?

MASON

Clinically? Oh no, no—

HARPER

I want to be close to you.

MASON

No you don't.

HARPER

How can you say that?

MASON

Because I'm not close to myself.

HARPER

Can I just hold your hand?

MASON

No.

HARPER

Please.

MASON

No.

HARPER

Do you respect me?

MASON

Yes, in my own way.

HARPER

Then why are you treating me like this?

MASON

Because I don't have a choice.

HARPER

That's bullshit.

MASON

Being in the same room with you feels like being submerged; then, suddenly released from that engulfment—repeatedly.

HARPER

You're afraid of me.

MASON

What?

HARPER

You don't like how unequivocally I choose you—

MASON

Actually, that's right—

HARPER

But I don't want to be right about that!

MASON

I'm really incredibly simple, Harper, and I've been extraordinarily simple my whole life…I'm just worn down by having to explain myself in complicated terms; it's aging me: I feel older and older and older. I'm aging exponentially. My ability to recover is gone; it's just gone.

HARPER

I like your novel.

MASON

'Like.'

HARPER

Mason. You're fishing—

MASON

That's not what I'm doing—

HARPER

You want me to call you a genius—

MASON

A lump of animal brain composed Mozart's
music; remember that: there was divine activity
in something fleshly.

HARPER

I don't believe in God—

MASON

You are my means for achieving grace; do you
know that?

HARPER

Talking to you is like listening to an orchestra
tune up.

MASON

I know—

HARPER

But it's such desperate music.

MASON

It's the revision of what is really an experience of
being at a loss, while remaining at the mercy of
the infinite calculus of language.

HARPER

What are you talking about?

MASON

I'm talking about a lifetime of self-willed
forgetting.

HARPER

You remember everything. You write me emails that tell me what I ate for breakfast two years ago.

MASON

Which is exactly why forgetting has to be willed—

HARPER

That's ridiculous—

MASON

Anaesthesia, that's one technique: if it hurts invent a different pain.

HARPER

Oh just shut up—

MASON

Do you think of yourself as a moral person—

HARPER

Sure.

MASON

What about your friends? Do you consider them to be moral people?

HARPER

Some of them.

MASON

What about your parents?

HARPER
  Not really.

MASON
  What about me?

HARPER
  You hurt people—

MASON
  Maybe by accident—

HARPER
  You hurt me—

MASON
  Oops.

HARPER
  What about what your wife did to you?

MASON
  What about it?

HARPER
  Didn't that *pain* evolve into some kind of
  understanding, or empathy or something—

MASON
  Pain can't evolve. It's too basic.

HARPER
  You should know better. You should know what it
  feels like to be inexplicably abandoned.

MASON

You don't know anything about my marriage.

HARPER

Yes I do. You used to tell me all about it.

MASON

I told you stories; I didn't tell you about my
marriage.

HARPER

You won't ever admit to having been sincere with
me.

MASON

I wasn't though.

HARPER

But you were.

MASON

According to you.

HARPER

No: according to you; according to the way you
needed me; according to the way you used to
call me in the middle of the night and beg me to
sneak out and come over to see you; according
to the way you used to tell me to meet you
inbetween my classes, during my lunch break—
or—

MASON
　Harper, you're conflating things—

HARPER
　What am I conflating?

MASON
　My wanting to fuck you with my being sincere.

HARPER
　You say things that are so violent, even though
　you don't move a muscle while you speak.

MASON
　Yes, because maybe violence is the point; maybe
　it's necessary; immanent, even.

HARPER
　Do you enjoy scaring me?

MASON
　I'm not enjoying it, no.

HARPER
　I feel like you are.

MASON
　You misunderstand me then.

HARPER
　What don't I understand?

MASON

That I'm immured behind impenetrable
layers of self-doubt; self-injury; self-fulfilling
prophecies...

HARPER

Why don't you share any of that doubt with me
then? Maybe I could help you—

MASON

I doubt it.

HARPER

I know you better than anybody.

MASON

That's not saying much.

HARPER

You want to be more of a mystery than you really
are. It's a ploy, a bluff, a game.

MASON

It's a secret.

HARPER

My parents texted me: they're on their way.

MASON

Cool.

HARPER

So you should probably go—

MASON

We swim like electric eels at the bottom of this loneliness, trying not to shock each other…

HARPER

You're angry with me because of what happened with Alex—

MASON

I'm not angry.

HARPER

I literally just kissed him—

MASON

I'm not angry.

HARPER

Then what are you punishing me for?

MASON

I'm not punishing you.

HARPER

Yes you are.

MASON

I'm not punishing, I'm attempting.

HARPER

Attempting what?

MASON

To dig my way out of the pauper's grave before
I'm forcibly thrown back into it.

HARPER

I know that you're artistically dissatisfied, blah
blah blah—I don't wanna keep talking about the
same bullshit every day—

MASON

I always wished that I was a sensitive, gentle
person. A patient listener. But from a very early
age I got caught up in a kind of religious form
of mental torture that's done violence to the rest
of me. I live in the burrow I've dug for my own
suffocating sense of captivity and loneliness. I'm
animal, you know, caught in a world of people.

HARPER

I love you.

MASON

The miracle of language is its metaphorical
capacity to reverse what we live into what we feel.
To take an ocean outside and transform it into an
ocean within.

HARPER

I love you.

MASON

See what I mean?

HARPER

I need you to hear what I'm saying—

MASON

When very famous people die, the streets that follow the funeral procession are littered with poems—very bad ones mostly—because short stories are too long to read at funerals—

HARPER

Did you like waking up with me, here, this morning?

MASON

I forget.

HARPER

Do you think it's something you could do for the rest of your life?

MASON

Wake up with you?

HARPER

Yes—

MASON

I forget.

> *HARPER doesn't say anything.*

MASON

Silence between people almost always means that they're disappointed in one another—

HARPER

I still re-read your book. I've probably read it about twenty times—

MASON

Ok.

HARPER

Why are you so insecure about your writing?

MASON

I'm not insecure—

HARPER

Defensive—

MASON

No, not defensive either.

HARPER

What then?

MASON

Pissed.

HARPER

At whom?

MASON

Whomever decided to bury Mozart the way they did.

HARPER

Mason, I know you still care about me.

MASON

Another naive statement—

HARPER

Why is that naive?

MASON

Because I'm no longer interested in the contents
of my own feelings; for you or anyone—

HARPER takes out her phone and begins to scroll:

HARPER

I want to read you something.

MASON

Ok...

HARPER

Because it was your method of prayer that drew
my attention; the motion of your hands being
brought together like a family sitting down for
dinner. I am obsessed by the thought that I really
do love you, and that I love you in a way that
approaches happiness. But then I have this fear,
too, that there's a loophole in your affection for
me, and that I'm about to fall through it and thus
fall into nowhere, and so I wanted to write to you
to tell you that everything is perfect and that we
should just stand still for fear of falling from this
perfect place. I say this selfishly, but also because
I'm almost certain that you want to ask the same
of me: to stand still, to not betray the perfect
accidents of time and circumstance that brought
us here.

MASON

Who wrote that?

HARPER

You, in an email to me, five years ago.

MASON

Oh.

HARPER

You used to write me a lot of emails like that.

MASON

I wish I hadn't.

HARPER

You've taken so much from me—

MASON

Take as much of yourself back from me as you
want. Please. Then I'll be light enough to float;
because a man on his own is weightless; he has
no internal gravity—

HARPER

I didn't say I want you to give anything back—I
just said you've taken: and that you keep
taking...you should go, soon—

MASON

I plan on it.

HARPER

Something feels off.

MASON

Uhuh.

HARPER

We're not going to see each other again; after
this—

MASON

Doesn't seem like it.

HARPER

We're talking about six years of my life—

MASON

A few minutes ago, we were talking about the improbability of my getting a second erection this morning.

HARPER

It bothers you more than you admit—

MASON

What does?

HARPER

Your physical indifference to me.

MASON

Animal lust would be a neat solution to my problems, I'll admit.

HARPER

You don't have any real problems, only fake problems.

MASON

Define 'fake.'

HARPER

Problems you create yourself.

MASON

In that case, strictly speaking, you're correct.

HARPER

Why aren't you more upset?

MASON doesn't respond.

HARPER

Mason: why aren't you more upset?

MASON

Why would I be upset?

HARPER

Because we fell out of love—

MASON

Time passed, we eroded.

HARPER

Well can we de-erode?

MASON

I don't think geology works like that.

HARPER

I don't know how to talk myself into this business
of giving up. I just want you to dislodge me from
my emotional hiding place—but you're content
to send me postcards instead—

MASON

No, I don't send postcards because I don't know
the address. I send up flares from my own secret
refuge—

HARPER

Well I don't see them.

MASON
Look just past the horizon.

HARPER
We know too much about each other to really
talk to each other.

MASON
True.

HARPER
More and more we just exchange silences,
knowing silences even…but there's no banter, no
play, no joyfulness. It sucks. It fucking sucks.

MASON
You want your own identity—an indentity totally
independent of me—but you're not willing to do
the hard work to construct one.

HARPER
Get over yourself.

MASON
I'm telling you something important.

HARPER
See: that just sounds so so so smug to me.

MASON
It's purely empirical.

HARPER

What? It's 'purely empirical' to say that I have
no personality except through you? Go fuck
yourself—

MASON

Listen to me Harper—

HARPER

What?

MASON

It's not that you don't have a personality, it's just
that you think your personality sounds better
when you sing it in the cathedral of someone
else's ideas—

HARPER

Still. Smug. Still condescending. No, not even
condescending: imperious, regal, disdainful; self-
obsessed…I feel like you don't know anything
about me. It's like the longer we're together, the
less—

MASON

Are we together?

HARPER

The longer we're bonded—

MASON

Better—

HARPER

The less I know about you, and the more I want to know.

MASON

Because emotions are like the tide: they reverse—

HARPER

Constantly. They reverse constantly.

MASON

So why resist it?

HARPER

Because I have to suffer in an out-control-way—

MASON

You have to learnt to float above it—

HARPER

You want an impossible kind of innocence from me—it's not fair.

MASON

Not from you, from myself—

HARPER

Well good luck with that.

MASON

Do you want to have sex? Before I go—

HARPER
  Mason…

MASON
  Do you or don't you?

HARPER
  I don't know how to answer that question.

MASON
  With a 'yes' or a 'no.'

HARPER
  I haven't found our conversation to be
  particularly erotic—

MASON
  I have.

HARPER
  Are you psychotic?

MASON
  How would I know?

HARPER
  Do you really want to have sex?

MASON
  I want revealed truth.

HARPER
  Is that a 'no?'

MASON

I think it's closer to 'yes.'

HARPER starts to undress.

MASON

Literature begins with Achilles killing over lost love—

HARPER stops undressing.

MASON

Because how could literature begin except with grief?

HARPER

What are you grieving over, Mason?

MASON

I don't know.

HARPER

You should figure it out.

MASON

Love is a thought—

HARPER

Is this why you're not helping me undress?

MASON

That's part of it.

HARPER
And what's the other part?

MASON
You're trying to sanction pain—

HARPER
I'm trying to be honest with myself.

MASON
No, you're trying to sanction it—

HARPER
I don't know what you mean.

MASON
Just say that there's just pain—

HARPER
No.

MASON
There's the sanction then: there's the resistance—

HARPER
I'm not resisting—

MASON
You want to salvage me from anguish.

HARPER
I always feel like I'm not being sincere enough
with you—

MASON

No, you just wish your words had greater effect—

HARPER

I want to untangle my words from ambiguity—

MASON

Our world is threaded through with the tough
fiber of ambiguity.

HARPER

What world?

MASON

This physical, brutal one—

HARPER

You've made it brutal—

MASON

If you don't recognise that brutality is inherent to
being alive, to being a physical body, then you're
not being realistic, and you're going to be very,
very disappointed with the way your life turns
out—

HARPER

Everyone who knows you lives for the judgement
you've reserved for them.

MASON

Good.

HARPER
  You revel in it—

MASON
  Vaguely—

HARPER
  You need it.

MASON
  I don't.

HARPER
  You're obsessed with it.

MASON
  Not at all—

HARPER
  It's the only reason you sleep with me—

MASON
  So I can judge you?

HARPER
  Yes.

MASON
  For what?

HARPER
  Remaining separate from you. Refusing to
  merge. Taking my own pleasure.

MASON

Listen: I want to achieve the clean severence
we've both been lingering around to make—but
I can't because I physically don't want it; because
the pre-expressive, silent part of me doesn't want
a solitary mental life yet; abhors it actually and
will do anything to stop it from happening. Make
me leave in other words, because I want to leave;
but beg me to stay because I'm already begging.

HARPER

There's a part of you that always seems
incredibly young; like you're the youngest person
I know. But then sometimes, suddenly you
switch, and you're a bijallion years old and I don't
know how to be in the same room with you let
alone talk to you, because you resemble a grain
of sand or a rock out at sea more than a human
being.

MASON

It's easy to talk to a rock. You just throw it back
in the ocean.

HARPER

But you just crawl back ashore.

MASON

The waves carry me back: I don't have a choice.

HARPER

There's this concetrated purity in you...I've
never liked it; I always feel like I'm opening a
can of transcendentally sour milk. I want to just
hit you sometimes. I want to hit you all the time.
You're so hittable and weak in a way that totally
belies the fact that you're actually physically
quite strong. But what the fuck is it? What makes
you so stupidly fragile?—I never know.

MASON

Ah, you just have to put your hand on the heart
of self-possession; feel the ta-dum ta-dum ta
dum of it. Here here here. See? It's the spiritual
ticker: it doesn't like the job it's been given—it
wants to take a break, but it's technically not
allowed—

HARPER

I shouldn't ask you to explain anything.

MASON

People are so boring.

HARPER

What?

MASON

No, it's just that people are so fucking boring...
Not that you're boring Harper; you just tolerate
boring people too well.

HARPER

No, I tolerate them very badly. I just don't show it. Which is why I need you—

MASON

You don't need my misanthropy. It's very very ugly.

HARPER

I just need someone who can talk intelligently and get it up; two apparently antithetical qualities—

MASON

Intelligence tends to convert the erotic object into a purely poetic one; and the poetic object can't be closed up as neatly as the erotic object. It's a hygienic question really—the poetry of your body as it spills across the bed.

HARPER

I want to speak to people with the gorgeous logic of a poem, but I never seem to be able to. Instead I can only make harsh, metallic noises with my mouth.

MASON

Your repressed Puritanism makes sex a more harrowing experience than it should be, by the way.

HARPER

Sorry, how did you suddenly arrive at that conclusion?

MASON

I think the Puritanism comes from your Father, from what I can tell.

HARPER

I never talk about my father—

MASON

Exactly.

HARPER

I just wanted to have a simple time. Drink tea. Talk. Be kind. Be affectionate. Or just, be here to console each other over what we've lost over the years. But it's proved impossible—

MASON

The definition of an impossible object is something that can exist in two dimensions but can't exist in three.

HARPER

Am I an impossible object?

MASON

Do you exist in three-dimensions?

HARPER

Sometimes.

MASON

Well that makes it more complicated.

HARPER

I'm tired of things being complicated.

MASON

You have to find that thread that leads you out of the tricky voice of metaphor.

HARPER

You've just never lived a moment without control. I don't think you could suddenly give it up—

MASON

As a child, I talked to myself a lot, and with the plants and animals. I was convinced I could speak with everything. Animals knew who they were, but what about me?—I'd look at my hands and my feet and wonder what I should call myself... Everything was animated, and dark things lurked in the corners of the house to grab me and eat me—or so I thought. I lived near a power-plant, and sometimes I'd watch birds drop dead in the pollution from the smoke-stacks. My father left my mother for another man, and they never re-married. They are both still alive. My father read my book when it came out, and called me to tell me that he enjoyed it. My mother doesn't speak to me, because I still speak to my father...When I was very young, I imagined that I was prince who would inherit a great kingdom. Of course, as I got older, I began to realize that there was no kingdom, and that my only inheritance was what could be self-inflicted.

HARPER

Mason...

MASON

There's a gap between me and what's around me—

HARPER

Because you want there to be.

MASON

No, no: there just is.

HARPER

Once, I convinced my mother that I was
paralyzed from the waist down because I didn't
feel like attending kindergarten that morning.
It wasn't until my father came home that
someone thought to find out whether I was lying
by putting ice on my toes—my mother really
believed that I was telling the truth when I said
I'd lost all feeling in my legs.

MASON

Was she upset?

HARPER

Yes. But since then, she's never really trusted me.

MASON

You were five years old—

HARPER

Yet—to her—in that moment—I revealed that I
had a bad nature; that I was corrupt.

MASON

I think that story explains something very very
important about you, Harper.

HARPER

Sometimes I smell the laundry when it comes
out of the dryer and the dry heat of August
nights here and the sound of my brother's
laughter coming from the other room and I don't
know why I'm not happier; and I feel all the time
that you're a part of me, that you're always with
me: that I carry you with me wherever I go, on
the back of devotion—

MASON

A pearl falls asleep at the bottom of the
ocean; calls itself a soul. But when will the
soul remember that it's a pearl? That it's been
drowned for a thousand years?

HARPER

It's time for you to go, I think—

MASON

In a second.

HARPER

What are you waiting for?

MASON

This beautiful and mysterious disinterestedness
to pass.

HARPER

I don't think it will—

MASON

No, I don't think so either.

HARPER goes to the window. MASON watches her.

Exit MASON stage left.

Enter MASON, with winter-coat, hat, and gloves.

Exit MASON, stage center.

ACT II

Enter ELAINE and PAUL, each carrying small suitcases. They are followed by RYAN, with a backpack slung over his shoulder. RYAN exits immediately to his bedroom off-stage.

PAUL
Harper, we're here—

HARPER
(from off-stage)
Cool. I'm still working; I'll be out for lunch.

ELAINE
Why are you so hard on him, Paul?

PAUL
I'm not being hard on him—

ELAINE
Yes you are. You were on his case the entire car ride.

PAUL
Well, he never listens to me.

ELAINE
Why should he?

PAUL shakes his head.

.

PAUL

　Never mind.

ELAINE

　Whenever you're upset with me, you find a way
　to blame him—

PAUL

　The two of you gang up on me—

ELAINE

　I can understand why Harper wants to travel
　separately from the family...

PAUL

　She probably had one of her boyfriends over all
　weekend.

ELAINE

　Paul—

PAUL

　What? You don't think so?—

ELAINE

　I think she wanted to have some peace and quiet.

PAUL

　Whatever you say Elaine.

ELAINE

　Don't give me that—

PAUL

  I thought we came up here to relax—

    Enter RYAN, dressed to run, except with additional for the cold.

RYAN

  I'm going running on the beach.

ELAINE

  Ryan, it's freezing outside—

RYAN

  I'll be fine—

    Exit RYAN.

PAUL

  See—

ELAINE

  See what?

PAUL

  He has no common sense.

ELAINE

  He wants to go running—he's been in the car for three hours.

PAUL

  He's going to freeze his ass off out there—

ELAINE

  He's not going to die—

PAUL

  That's not the point—

ELAINE

  What's the point then?

PAUL

  That he should show some common sense!

ELAINE

  Just like you, right Paul?

PAUL

  Well—

ELAINE

  Because you've always made such sensible
  choices—

PAUL

  I didn't say that.

ELAINE

  That's what you implied—

PAUL

  He's my son—why would it be a bad thing if he
  did a few things the way I do them?—the simple
  things at least—

ELAINE

I don't know, maybe it wouldn't: but that's not
the point.

PAUL

What's the point then?

ELAINE

That you're too hard on him.

PAUL

Why do you protect him?

ELAINE

Why do you put me in a position where I have to
protect him?

PAUL

It's just what I do—ok?

ELAINE

We've already ruined Harper's peace and quiet.

PAUL

She's fine.

ELAINE

This family is incredible, sometimes.

PAUL

I didn't have to come with you and Ryan—

ELAINE

The four of us are never together.

PAUL

For good reason.

ELAINE

Oh yeah?

PAUL

Do you find it pleasant?—being together as a
family?

ELAINE

Do you?

PAUL

Not particularly.

ELAINE

I find that so sad—

PAUL

It's the truth.

ELAINE

It's depressing becoming one of those couples
that doesn't know how to function once their kids
have gone to college.

PAUL

That's not the only thing that's depressing.

ELAINE

I'm not in the mood for one of your threatening
allusions—

PAUL

Ok, then let me rephrase: it's depressing that we're pretending like you're not having an affair, when we both know you are.

ELAINE

Paul—we agreed—

PAUL

It's not like they're not going to find out—

ELAINE

Paul—

PAUL

Harper doesn't care—

ELAINE

How do you know?

PAUL

We already talked about it.

ELAINE

No, you didn't.

PAUL

Yes, we did. I talked to her on the phone about it. She's fine.

ELAINE

We haven't even separated yet—

PAUL
Technically, no, we haven't.

ELAINE
We agreed that we wouldn't say anything…. You agreed that you wouldn't say anything—

PAUL
I lied—and you're in no position to judge me for that, are you?

ELAINE
No. I'm not.

PAUL
We should unpack.

ELAINE
Don't unpack.

PAUL
Why not? I want to enjoy myself—

ELAINE
I want you to drive back, I'll go back with Ryan and Harper.

PAUL
I'm here. It's my house. I want to relax.

ELAINE
How can you possibly relax at this point?

PAUL

By being by myself.

ELAINE

It's not that big of a house.

PAUL

If none of us speak to each other, things should
be fine.

ELAINE

I intend on speaking to my family—

PAUL

Tactical error—

ELAINE

Give me a break. You're so happy to have the
moral high ground; it's fairly grotesque—

PAUL

I didn't choose to be in this position—

ELAINE

That's one interpretation.

PAUL

You're saying I forced you to have an affair?

ELAINE

That's one interpretation.

PAUL

Are any other interpretations available?

ELAINE

  I don't know, you tell me—

PAUL

  I'll leave that for you to decide.

ELAINE

  You have this passive way of shaming me—you
  always have.

PAUL

  Right. Because I forced you to break up our
  marriage—

ELAINE

  I forgave you for your affair.

PAUL

  What?

ELAINE

  What? Do you actually think I didn't know?

PAUL

  Excuse me?

ELAINE

  You don't think I know that you started sleeping
  with one of your graduate students—

PAUL

  What are you talking about?

ELAINE

I forget her name; the one with frizzy hair and the bouncy breasts; she's been at a few of our Christmas parties.

PAUL

I honestly don't know what you're talking about.

ELAINE

Yes you do. You're a bad liar. But that doesn't matter; the point is: I found a way to forgive you.

PAUL

I don't know who you're talking about.

ELAINE

You're really not going to be honest with me?

PAUL

You weren't honest with me.

ELAINE

I let myself be caught—

PAUL

You're saying that after the fact—

ELAINE

People have affairs because they want to be caught.

PAUL

I disagree.

ELAINE

Does it upset you that I overlooked your affair
while you tried to destroy me for mine? My
apologies—

PAUL

I never slept with one of my graduate students.

ELAINE

Oh but you slept with other women right?

PAUL

I never said that!

ELAINE

But you do sleep with your graduate students.
You're sleeping with one right now. Like I said,
I remember her well; I just forget her name.
She chain-smokes and talks incessantly about
Nietzsche and always hits herself in the face with
her breasts. It's embarrassing for everyone—

PAUL

Where are you getting this from?

ELAINE

You left a note from her in the pocket of your
jeans a few weeks ago. And then I did some
homework. Like I said, people who have affairs
want to get caught.

PAUL

Lizzy. Her name's Lizzy.

ELAINE

Thank you Paul. I'm sure you feel relieved.

PAUL

I'm not relieved.

ELAINE

It hasn't hit you yet, then.

PAUL

Don't talk to me.

ELAINE

I mean, I was relieved when you found out about—

PAUL

I don't want to continue this conversation right now—

ELAINE

I loved not having to conceal how much I enjoyed being touched by someone else—

PAUL

Privacy means nothing to you, does it?

ELAINE

Not at the moment.

PAUL

I wanted to leave you years ago. But I didn't.
Because I knew you couldn't handle being alone.
Not at least until you'd found someone else to
put up with your endless, neurotic bullshit—

ELAINE

I gave up painting for you Paul. I stayed at home
while you were working on getting tenure. I
asked my parents for money so that we could
afford to live the way we have—

PAUL

What's your point?

ELAINE

My point is that you're acting like your
remaining in the marriage was some kind of
noble act of self-sacrifice—

PAUL

You brought me here to trap me—

ELAINE

In a way.

PAUL

This a show-trial for the kids.

ELAINE

Harper doesn't care—

PAUL

You've already told her, didn't you?

ELAINE

A long time ago.

PAUL

Fuck.

ELAINE

Are you afraid to hear what she thinks?

PAUL

It makes me uncomfortable.

ELAINE

Why have an affair then—if you're uncomfortable
with the title of adulterer?

PAUL

What about Ryan?

ELAINE

Ryan and Harper talk—

PAUL

Jesus Christ.

ELAINE

Don't look so astonished. It doesn't make a
difference whether the kids know or not.

PAUL

I'm their father—

ELAINE

Nominally.

PAUL

What does that mean?—I've been a good father
to them, and you know that—

ELAINE

Maybe with Harper you were. She forgave you,
by the way, in case you were wondering. I'm not
sure about Ryan—

PAUL

Why did you get married to me?

ELAINE

Because I was in love with you. Because I wanted
to have your children.

PAUL

And I disappointed you?

ELAINE

Gradually.

PAUL

Is nothing left of that love?—assuming it was
real—

ELAINE

That kind of love never completely goes away; it
doesn't just die—

PAUL

Love can always die.

ELAINE

That's a man's perspective—

PAUL

No, it's a universal perspective: people are finite, emotions are finite. It's the fragility of love that's exciting in the first place—

ELAINE

Again, a man's perspective.

PAUL

I used to listen to my parents fight, as a kid, and I hated it; I thought it was horrific. And now I think about Ryan, Harper listening to us, and what they must think—

ELAINE

This is what married people become—get over it.

PAUL

It shouldn't be that way.

ELAINE

Look, Paul, you were never really interested in the details of family life. It was always too messy, too unphilosophical, too disappointing. But I've been doing all the cleaning up—

PAUL

That's just your negative fantasy; that's just what your using as justification—

ELAINE

You beckon someone, you touch their face, you kiss them—that's adultery. Ok?—there's no justification: it's just something that happens—you know that.

PAUL

I guess I do.

ELAINE

You're so susceptible to self-knowledge—and for someone who teaches philosophy—

PAUL

What about you Elaine?—are you impervious?

ELAINE

No, I'm not impervious.

PAUL

Then there are things about yourself you don't like to hear, right?

ELAINE

Yes, there are.

PAUL

And do I go out of my way to say them? Do I rub salt in your wounds?

ELAINE

No, you're too indifferent.

PAUL

Maybe I'm just too kind.

ELAINE

You're saying that checking-out emotionally is a form of kindness? Are you really saying that?

PAUL

I'm saying that love, commitment, family, is easier the less you think about it; the less you offer critical perspectives about it while it's happening; but all I have are critical perspectives...so there's got to be some kind of distance, for me—

ELAINE

That's bullshit.

PAUL

It's an honest approximation—

ELAINE

Of what?

PAUL

Of me. Of, I don't know, how marriages work,
or have to work in order to survive—I mean,
listen, you never took criticism well Elaine; but
you always loved to offer it. You're always noting
things I do wrong, you always file them away for
a moment when they're particularly useful—like
you did just now. Just like you'll keep doing. But
you can't stand, you just can't stand to be treated
by people the way you treat them. And I've
always recognized that. I've always let you off
the hook. I've let myself get beat up emotionally
without hitting back—and all I've asked in
return is to be allowed a sphere that's entirely
my own—for a little solitude; for a little of the
privacy that's necessary for any mature adult
human being—

ELAINE

I don't give a fuck about your opinion of me
Paul. Criticize me as much as you want—

PAUL

You only say that because you have someone
else—

ELAINE

You can't intimidate me.

PAUL

Imagine if I could, though—

ELAINE

Everything's so different—

PAUL

What is?

ELAINE

From the first time we came up here, years ago—

PAUL

That's obvious.

ELAINE

Don't look at me like I owe you some kind of
sympathy.

PAUL

We haven't slept together in two years—

ELAINE

So what?

PAUL

You won't touch me—

ELAINE

So what?

PAUL

You choked the life out of our marriage—

ELAINE

Choking would have been more erotic than what
we had—

Enter HARPER.

HARPER

Can you two please shut up!?

Exit HARPER, door slams off-stage.

PAUL

And if you didn't have someone else you wouldn't be nearly so assertive, would you? You don't do anything that isn't tactical, strategic, pragmatic—

ELAINE

Isn't that the exact kind of thing you said I couldn't bear to hear?

PAUL

It is—

ELAINE

Well I can bear it. See. Still in one piece.

PAUL

Another tactic—

ELAINE

Remaining in one piece?

PAUL

You're displaying a strength that isn't there.

ELAINE

That's what you'd like to think—

PAUL
A delayed breakdown is still a breakdown.

ELAINE
I'm not delaying anything—

PAUL
Except for your fury, which you'll save for
Harper, in a moment when I'm not there—

ELAINE
Right, because you need to feel like Harper hates
me as much as Ryan hates you—

PAUL
I don't 'need to feel' anything; it's just what you
do—you take advantage of the fact that Harper
doesn't fight back—

ELAINE
She fights back by ignoring me—

PAUL
As she has every right to—

ELAINE
Even though you demand that Ryan does
everything you say.

PAUL
That's a different situation—

ELAINE
Hypocrite—

PAUL

Ryan has more growing up to do than Harper—

ELAINE

I saw the way you reacted when he brought his boyfriend home for Thanksgiving—

PAUL

That's not relevant.

ELAINE

It seemed relevant then, to you.

PAUL

Just because I wasn't comfortable—

ELAINE

What was there to be comfortable with?

PAUL

I'm not sure—

ELAINE

You saw his image diverging from yours; you saw him becoming some other than who you imagined he'd be—

PAUL

I my son kissing another man—

ELAINE

Yes and do you remember what you said?

PAUL

No.

ELAINE

Then I won't repeat it.

PAUL

Good.

ELAINE

You called him "a little—

PAUL

Don't—

ELAINE

At least Harper is on your side, right?

PAUL

Why don't we just not say anything for a second?

   Pause.

ELAINE

I used to love the vacations we took to this
house. When the twins were little. And we'd sit
on the deck and watch the fireworks and you'd
take home-videos; when we'd make love after the
kids had gone to sleep and night and stars had
settled over the water. And when...and when I
still had faith that all my doubts about myself
and about you would resolve themselves into
something truly unimpeachable and whole and—

PAUL

There's so much we've never talked about Elaine.
I don't even know how to begin.

ELAINE

Self-recognition is an emancipatory move, which
is why married people avoid it...

PAUL

What do you think we've been avoiding?

ELAINE

Everything that could give rise to a sense of
shame or self-hatred.

PAUL

I don't lack for shame or self-hatred.

ELAINE

Which is why you can't love me the way I need
to be loved.

PAUL

You're endlessly in the process of making one
piece of me into the whole thing. You just don't
let go of any observation, any detail—

ELAINE

But the details of a person are infinite. One little
thing—it goes on forever.

PAUL

Don't you think that…that marrying someone—
don't you think that it means surrendering those
infinities; or accepting them; that it just means
letting people off the hook?

ELAINE

I don't know. Maybe that's what marriage should
mean. But that's not what it means for me.

PAUL

What does it mean then?

ELAINE

Obviously, I have no idea anymore…. It's
a burden—to continually have to prove the
authenticity of choices made at twenty-two—

PAUL

Why do we have to prove anything? why can't
we just hold each other and…and forgive each
other; start over—

ELAINE

You're too sentimental—

PAUL doesn't respond.

ELAINE

Did I hurt your feelings?

PAUL

You're the one who told that story about coming
to the house when the kids were little—

ELAINE

Yes, but I wasn't being sentimental.

PAUL

Yes you were!

ELAINE

I was mourning, there's a difference.

PAUL

You don't think I'm mourning right now?

ELAINE

No. Not at all.

PAUL

Then what am I doing?

ELAINE

Pretending that you'd do things differently, given
a second chance, when, in fact, you'd do things the
exact same way you did them the first time.

PAUL

So would you—

ELAINE

Oh no no no: I'd do everything differently, right from the beginning; right from the moment I was born as a lonely baby. I'd have swallowed my first gasps of air differently—

PAUL

How can you expect me to love you if you don't love anything?

ELAINE

Good question.

PAUL

Because despite whatever shit you accuse me of—despite whatever shit I'm guilty of—I can actually fall in love with things.

ELAINE

You love being adored by younger women. So when I was a younger woman who adored you, you loved me. And now that I'm not, you don't.

PAUL

You're relentless.

ELAINE

Because that's what I need to be right now.

A pause.

PAUL

You're better at the politics of confession than I
am—

ELAINE

I'm more comfortable with my own truths—

PAUL

What truths?

ELAINE

I have a strength that's deeper in me than my
circumstances; than my age—

PAUL

All you're saying is that you can still attract men—

ELAINE

Younger men, even—

PAUL

Go to hell.

ELAINE

Why does that bother you more than if I'd said,
'older?'

PAUL

Oh it doesn't fucking matter—

ELAINE

Clearly it bothers you.

PAUL

Just like Lizzy bothers you.

ELAINE

It isn't the fact that she's twenty-four—

PAUL

Then what is it?

ELAINE

I already told you: it's the fact that you keeping
repeating the same erotic fantasy, over and over.
It's a fact that Lizzy is one of many twenty-four
year olds. One in a series, unique in some ways,
but generic in others.

PAUL

If you don't take my erotic life seriously, then why
do you expect me to talk about it?

ELAINE

Because I'm tired of this hygienic separation of
words and what we actually do—

PAUL

So am I!

ELAINE

Ok then.

PAUL

I don't know what to say next...

ELAINE

You had an office Paul, you rented a studio so that
you could have your precious contemplative space.
But what you really had was your own life, your
own escape from the actual responsibilities you'd
committed yourself to as a father—

PAUL

You had a house-keeper, a nanny which your
parents paid for. I mean, give me a break—

ELAINE

You only think of child-rearing in terms of the
physical stuff you have to do. But it wasn't you
that Harper talked to when she lost her virginity;
it wasn't you that Ryan came out to—

PAUL

This kind of hostility doesn't touch me.

ELAINE

What does touch you then Paul?

PAUL

Something that's more than skin deep—

ELAINE

Your children don't share anything with you for a
reason—

PAUL

Harper shares things with me.

ELAINE
> She feels bad for you, so she reaches out from
> time to time. But it's really just pity.

PAUL
> I don't want to believe that.

ELAINE
> You wanted something more than 'skin deep'—

PAUL
> Well, I got it—ok?

ELAINE
> You have a hard time imagining yourself as
> pitiable—

PAUL
> Pity displaces love—

ELAINE
> It does—

PAUL
> So you're saying my family doesn't love me?

ELAINE
> You're vain and you're stubborn—

PAUL
> Those aren't good enough reasons—

ELAINE
> I'm sure your children love you Paul, relax.

PAUL

What about the first summer we bought this
house?—you spent the whole summer trying
to ingratiate yourself with the women from the
yacht club and basically ignored the kids—

ELAINE

Why are you bringing that up?

PAUL

Because you're pious without warrant.

ELAINE

I'm not pious, Paul; I'm not pious at all—I'm just
telling you the places where I'm weak and the
places where I'm strong—and you can figure out
the rest for yourself.

PAUL

You always conceal your judgements within
your observations; you act like you're just cooly,
dispassionately telling me 'things' about myself,
about our marriage, about you—but you're really
trying to win. You're trying to win the end of our
marriage—

ELAINE

Yes, to make up for your winning the beginning
of it—

PAUL

How could I possibly have 'won' the beginning of
our marriage?

ELAINE

Oh, I don't know? By convincing me that
matrimonial bondage was what was best for me—

PAUL

How could I possibly have done that?

ELAINE

By pretending to be something that you
weren't—

PAUL

Which was what?

ELAINE

Someone capable of genuine, loving affection.

PAUL

Oh come on—

ELAINE

No: that's what I wanted: I wanted tenderness,
for life; not for a year. And that's what I thought
I was signing up for.

PAUL

This whole afternoon you've been busily
connecting each and every node of pain, wire by
wire, until the moment when you could flip on
the electricity—

Enter HARPER.

HARPER

Can you two PLEASE be quiet? I'm so tired of
your stupid fights!

PAUL

Why don't you sit down here with us Harper?

ELAINE

Paul, she doesn't want to have to listen to us.

HARPER

I can speak for myself—I didn't say I didn't want
to listen. I said I didn't want to listen to you
at this volume. Or I should say: at this level of
bullshit.

ELAINE

Fine, would you like to join the conversation?

HARPER

What could I possibly add?

PAUL

Have you been listening to everything?

HARPER

I've been trying not to, but certain things have forced their way into my brain.

ELAINE

Like what?

HARPER

Basically, the fact that my parents hate each other.

ELAINE

We don't hate each other—

HARPER

Then what do you call this?

ELAINE

We're fighting.

HARPER

It's not fighting, it's a war of annihilation.

ELAINE

Harper, you're being dramatic.

HARPER

Don't be patronizing—

ELAINE

I'm not being patronizing—

HARPER

Yes you are—

ELAINE
No, I'm just not going to put up with being told
that this is a normal fight—

PAUL
Unfortunately, this is what has become normal
fight for us, Harper—

ELAINE
Harper, have you been crying?—your eyes are all
red—

HARPER
Don't worry about that right now.

ELAINE
This our fault Paul—

HARPER
Mom! It has nothing to do with you.

ELAINE
So you admit that something's wrong—

HARPER
Yes! But it doesn't matter.

ELAINE
You worry me Harper—

HARPER

No, I'm just the nearest and most convenient excuse to stop worrying about your own—very obvious—problems, at least until Ryan gets back from his run.

PAUL

Harper, give your mother a break—

HARPER

Ok Dad, how about we talk about you then? About how you've kind of been a creep to Mom—

PAUL

Please don't say that...

HARPER

I hate how no man will ever just show an emotion—his emotion.

ELAINE

Harper, I'm not sure this is helpful...

HARPER

I'm not trying to be helpful! I'm trying to represent to you people how pissed off I am—

ELAINE

Just tell me what's got you so upset, I mean, other than us—

HARPER

You haven't earned the right to know.

ELAINE

To know what?

HARPER

The sorrowful texture of my inner-life.

ELAINE

Oh, I'm so worried; I can't help it.

PAUL

Can everybody just calm down?

ELAINE/HARPER

No!

PAUL

Alright, alright—

HARPER

Why did you have to come up here this weekend?
We're all happiest when we're apart—

ELAINE

We miss you, when you're at school—

HARPER

Can you and Dad can stop referring to
yourselves as 'we'—please?

ELAINE

I miss you. Your father misses you.

HARPER

Yeah, you miss having an audience for your blow-
outs—

ELAINE

We do our best—

HARPER

Do your best to what?

ELAINE

Be civil.

HARPER

But why? What's the point?—

PAUL

Because we care about you and your brother.

HARPER

No more 'we!'

PAUL

Fine: both of us care, individually, about our
children.

HARPER

And you show it by taking us on a vacation where
you freak the fuck out the second you arrive?
What I don't get is why you bother to keep up
this front of civility in the first place? Like why
pretend like you're not planning these trips as
anything other than a total bloodletting?

PAUL

Because—

HARPER

Because what?

PAUL

I don't know…

ELAINE

Because we don't know what else to do.

HARPER

Ryan and I are old enough to deal with it—ok?
We're both in college; we're both out of the
nest—honestly: neither of us cares what the two
of you do; I think you're just clinging out to the
dream of family life mattering—

ELAINE

It does matter, to me—

HARPER

I don't see why.

PAUL

Because it just does. You'd understand if you had
kids.

HARPER

Dad, I really don't have any clue why or how you
teach philosophy. You are the most conventional
asshole in the universe.

PAUL

This has nothing to do with convention.

HARPER

What does it have to do with then?

PAUL

Human decency, human care—

HARPER

Those are conventions!

PAUL

They're all we've got kiddo—

HARPER

I'm not in the mood to be called 'kiddo.'

ELAINE

Harper—what's going on in your head? Will you
please tell me? I've never seen you like this—

HARPER

Like what?—angry?

ELAINE

Yes...

HARPER

Get used to it.

ELAINE

Ok...

HARPER
See you and Dad both screwed other people,
so neither of you can really feel self-righteous;
but I haven't done anything to anyone: so I feel
justified in saying just about anything right
now—

PAUL
Is there something in particular that you'd like to
tell us?

HARPER
No, not really.

HARPER thinks about it.

HARPER

Well. Now that I think about it: it's *so* selfish;
how the two of you are dragging out the process
of getting separated, because neither one of you
is willing to appear as manipulative, dishonest,
or cruel as you really are; at heart. It's not about
the fact that you've both had affairs: it's about the
way you both instrumentalize the ideal of family
happiness in order to hide your flaws; how you
both depend upon the machinary of family-life
to produce your self-esteem; your identity.... It's
all I can think about while I listen to you gossip
and yell and flirt and accuse, accuse, accuse: that
my presence is being taken advantage of. That
my attentativeness, my good-daughterness, my
listening-ears... are being abused for the sake
of giving the two of you some semblance of
coherence and purpose. But enough's a fuckin'
'nough.

Enter RYAN.

RYAN

Goddamn, it's cold outside. I'm going to take a
shower.

Exit RYAN.

HARPER

I'd honestly allowed myself to forget how
poisonous our family environment is until this
afternoon reminded me—

ELAINE

Do you really think we're that bad?

HARPER

No Mom—I think we're probably like everyone
else is: which is an even more miserable
thought—

PAUL

I think it's time to end this discussion for now—

ELAINE

You're making me feel so desperate—both of
you—

HARPER

Oh god, now she's crying—

PAUL

Why are you being so hard on your mother,
Harper?

HARPER

You've got to be kidding—

PAUL

You're upsetting your mother on purpose.

HARPER

You graduated from the school of betraying people in secret, Dad, so I can understand why open warfare makes you uncomfortable—

PAUL

Elaine, are you ok?

ELAINE

I'm fine. I'm fine. Please don't touch me—

HARPER

Why don't we all have a drink?

PAUL

Are you smiling?

HARPER

Well, it's kinda funny—

PAUL

What is 'kinda funny?'

HARPER

How ridiculous we all are—

PAUL

I don't find it funny.

Enter RYAN in a towel, ready for a shower.

RYAN

Because you utterly lack a sense of humor.

Exit RYAN.

PAUL

I don't appreciate being talked to like this by my
children.

HARPER

You were so much fun when I was young. You
played music, and danced, and threw parties. You
were always reading to me and taking me to films
I was too young to understand. You introduced
me to your friends and your students—you were
so alive, really: you were my example of a truly
alive person.

PAUL

People change.

HARPER

But why?

PAUL

They just do—

HARPER

I'm serious—I want to know why—

PAUL

Life takes things from you as you age; you can't
understand that now.

HARPER

I'm perfectly capable of understanding, if you'd
just explain—

PAUL

I can't.

HARPER

Maybe because you don't want to admit that you
had a choice to become something more than a
prematurely worn-out, emotionally numb old
fart.

ELAINE

Your father is fifty-five years old Harper, that's
hardly—

HARPER

Old fart is old fart, it's not a biological thing
necessarily.

PAUL

You're right, Harper, about my not being the
person that I used to be.

HARPER

You're gonna go on to explain how much you've
sacrificed so much for this family, right?—

PAUL

Until you've been a parent, don't—

HARPER

But that's the line you're about to give, right?
Like: 'I became a bitter, ungiving person, blah
blah blah; but I had to work really really hard to
make tenure so that justifies it blah blah blah; I
wanted more money and prestige and it cost me
blah blah blah.'

PAUL

That's not fair—

HARPER

Fair is whatever's true.

ELAINE

Harper, maybe you should go back to working on
your paper—

HARPER

You're both such babies. All you talk about is how
much you miss me, how you can't wait to see me,
blah blah blah; but then I start to actually share
what I think with you—

PAUL

Harper, I'm not sure what you think you're
doing, but it isn't making anything better—

HARPER
There's nothing to make better. Our family's totally fucked. It's just a matter of sorting out who gets what stuff and how much Ryan and I will feel like talking to either of you.

ELAINE
Please, please don't say things like that—

HARPER
I feel like I'm the only grown up in the room.

ELAINE
I love all of you so much.

PAUL
Do you?

ELAINE
Yes.

HARPER
What's the point of talking about love if you can't live up to it?

ELAINE
I'm trying Harper—

HARPER

I just want to know when my family is gonna stop living like life is eternal and recognize that if we screw up this life we have together—or had—that we're not gonna get it back; that there's no mechanism for getting it back.

ELAINE

No, there isn't, is there?

PAUL

Elaine, I'm going back to New York. You and Ryan can take Harper's car.

ELAINE

I'm coming with you.

PAUL

I prefer that you stay.

ELAINE

Fine...

PAUL picks up his bag and heads to the door.

ELAINE

Paul—

PAUL

I just need to do some thinking.

Exit PAUL stage center.

ELAINE
  Why did you have to get involved in the
  argument?

HARPER
  Why did you have to get married?

ELAINE
  That's a good question.

HARPER
  I feel bad for both of you.

ELAINE
  I know it's tough having to come home to see
  your family, when you're in college—

HARPER
  It shouldn't have to be this terrible though—

  Enter PAUL.

PAUL
  Harper, why is your old high school English
  teacher standing outside our house?

HARPER
  Which one; I had several high-school English
  teachers—

PAUL
  Harper—

  Exit HARPER stage left.

Sound of door slamming.

PAUL and ELAINE look at each other. They do not move.

ACT III

HARPER, RYAN, and ELAINE sit on the floor,
with a wine bottle between them.

ELAINE

I'm getting worried—

RYAN

Dad just needs to drive around the block another
hundred or two-hundred times—

HARPER

What if something happened?

RYAN

What are you worried about Harper?—they're
just talking.

HARPER

It's so unnerving.

RYAN

Relax—

HARPER

Oh great advice Ryan, thank you—

RYAN

You can't control what happens—

HARPER

I've noticed.

ELAINE

I just wish you would have said something earlier Harper.

HARPER

What was I supposed to say?

RYAN

You were supposed to admit that you embody the whole psychology of romantic self-sacrifice. It would have allowed the rest of us to place you in a context in which you made sense—

ELAINE

Where do you get these things from?

RYAN

My brain. But look: Harper you needed something to happen, because you were obsessed with this person—you *are* obsessed with this person—

HARPER

You're the obsessive one, obviously: studying every single fucking thing I say or do; looking for signs of a breakdown—

ELAINE

It is a relief though, isn't it—that you don't have to keep anything a secret anymore?

HARPER

No it's not a relief. It feels like my relationship had a heart-attack.

RYAN

A heart-attack can be a relief—if you want to die, I mean.

HARPER

I don't know how to imagine being with him if it's not an incredibly private thing—

ELAINE

Maybe you shouldn't imagine being with him at all.

HARPER

Choose your words carefully—

ELAINE

I just wish you'd confided in me earlier.

HARPER

Mom, what was I supposed to say? Like, imagine being me, at sixteen. What am I supposed to tell my family? Like hey, heads up everyone: I'm sleeping with my English teacher and sometimes we fuck in his office and we talk about getting married when I'm legal—

ELAINE

Well, when you put it like that—

RYAN
  I knew.

HARPER
  What?

RYAN
  I read your diaries.

        HARPER screams and hits RYAN.

HARPER
  Faggot!

RYAN
  Lay off—

HARPER
  Asshole!

RYAN
  Who cares? I didn't tell anyone.

HARPER
  Still!

ELAINE
  You knew this whole time Ryan?

RYAN
  Yeah.

HARPER
  Fucker.

RYAN

And you gave it away in a million different ways, anyway. I'm surprised Mom and Dad didn't notice—

ELAINE

I noticed Harper was changing, but I didn't realize—

HARPER

What do you think that you noticed Mom?

ELAINE

I just thought you were growing up; that you were worried about whether boys liked you—I didn't realize—

HARPER

That I was in an adult relationship?

ELAINE

Right, I missed that.

HARPER

It's an easy thing to miss—

ELAINE

A mother should know these things.

HARPER

Why though?

ELAINE

Because I could have helped you.

HARPER

No one could have helped me.

RYAN

That's so ominous sounding.

HARPER

So?

RYAN

Was it really that dark?

HARPER

Sometimes. Yes.

RYAN

I don't believe you.

HARPER

You were reading my diaries, so you already have whatever answers you want.

RYAN

Unless you aren't the kind of person who writes down everything they feel.

HARPER

What do you think?

RYAN

I think you only write down a tenth of what you actually feel.

HARPER

What are you basing that on?

RYAN

Intuition.

HARPER

Ryan, I would have told you if you'd asked—

RYAN

What would I have asked?—'Hey, Harp, bang
any of your favorite educators today?'

HARPER

Maybe if you'd just actually asked me what was
bothering me—

ELAINE

Harper, I've asked you that a million times over
the years—

HARPER

Nagging me and asking me a sincere question
aren't the same thing.

ELAINE

You can be so cutting—

HARPER

Where do you think I learned it from?

ELAINE

Me.

HARPER

That's right. A skill which, ironically, I could
never employ with Mason.

ELAINE

You let him walk all over you, don't you—

HARPER

I just can't hurt him back—and I've tried.

RYAN

You wanted to penetrate and expose the fiction
of love—but you couldn't, you couldn't—so
instead, you stayed in love with the fiction of
love.

HARPER

Are you drunk?

RYAN

I hate that question.

ELAINE

He's not drunk—

HARPER

Then what the hell is he talking about?

RYAN

I'm talking about the paradoxes you build out
of straight forward propositions. For instance,
Mom—why didn't you realize that I was the one
who was worried about whether boys liked me or
not—and not Harper?

ELAINE

I don't know Ryan.

HARPER

Why did you guys have to come up here this
weekend?

RYAN

Why did you decide to make tender love to a
well-known novelist in your parent's vacation
home?

HARPER

He's not well-known.

RYAN

He should be though.

HARPER

Have you read his books?

RYAN

Mason was my teacher too—

HARPER

What's your point?

RYAN

My point is that I that know what he's like, too.

HARPER

Excuse me?

RYAN

Oh don't worry, this isn't where I drop the sick
revelation that I've been having an affair with my
sister's already illicit lover. I mean, *I am*, but it's
all in my imagination. And your diaries. Which
I'm grateful for, by the way. I was so happy
when you started to write about your sex life—

HARPER

You're in love with him...

RYAN

In love with him? Well, yes. From afar. He
shatters me.

ELAINE

Ryan this isn't the time—

RYAN

The time for what? Homoerotic fantasy? He's
just a mile away, circling the block like a bird of
prey. I think it's the perfect time—

HARPER

You're on his side—

RYAN

I'm on my side.

HARPER

This is torture.

RYAN

Harper, you've got to learn to love Mason outside of the vacuum you've created around him.

HARPER

I don't see why.

RYAN

Because. Because. Because.

HARPER

Because what?

RYAN

There's something about him that's extremely good. Unattainably good. And you have to see that *that,* that *goodness* isn't just yours: it's something that everyone who meets him wants to understand and yes, taste, and touch. It's erotic, being around him. And you want to, have to believe, that you're the only young woman, or young man, who ever attracted him; whoever felt special because of him. Which is why you seal him off from everybody else. Your family, your peers. Your brother. But it's a fantasy, a very dull one. And Mason knows it, which is why he waited patiently in the freezing cold for someone in the family to notice him. You think you're saving your relationship, but you're mummifying it; you think his showing up here is the worst thing that could have happened, but it's the only thing that could have happened. It's what you've driven him too. Whether or not either of you realizes it.

HARPER

You're supposed to hate him. You're supposed to want to fight him—

RYAN

Yes and I'm also supposed to prefer eating pussy to eating cock—

HARPER

You're not supposed to identify with him or
empathize with him or even think about him;
you're just supposed to react, like Dad—

ELAINE

Why don't we change the subject?

RYAN

To what? What other topics are possibly
available?

ELAINE

I have no idea—anything—

RYAN

Realistically—Mason is the only thing we're
going to be talking about in this family for a long
time.

HARPER

I hate that.

RYAN

Don't you enjoy the drama a little bit though?

HARPER

No, I don't.

RYAN

You're lying.

HARPER

Shut up.

RYAN
    You're impressed with yourself. You're infinitely
    pleased to have hooked such an existentially
    tortured fish—

HARPER
    This is jealousy speaking—

RYAN
    Only if he's good in bed. I wonder if he's a top
    or bottom?

HARPER
    Oh gross.

RYAN
    I bet he's a bottom—what fun—

ELAINE
    Can I intervene here?

RYAN / HARPER
    No!

ELAINE
    Fine.

HARPER
    I'm tired of having to be called as a witness
    against myself.

RYAN
    Then stop making everything you say a self-
    conscious allusion to your own sense of shame.

HARPER
  Ryan. Shut. Up.

ELAINE
  Ryan, this is upsetting—

RYAN
  Holy shit Mom, we're twenty-two years old. We
  can have serious disagreements—

ELAINE
  Are you having a serious disagreement right
  now?

RYAN
  Yes. There's an important difference of
  interpretation.

HARPER
  Which is what?

RYAN
  I'm insisting that we interpret what's just
  happened and you insist on getting drunk on the
  floor with Mom.

HARPER
  Make him stop—

ELAINE
  I can't.

RYAN
  Why can't we just talk openly—

HARPER

I can't even begin to be open about this—and it kills me that you read my diary—I can't believe that you expect me to trust you Ryan—

RYAN

I read that shit for your sake.

HARPER

How was your invading my privacy for 'my sake?'

RYAN

I wanted to know why you were showing all these micro-signs of being confused or miserable or something. And because I honestly suspected what was going on. Again, I mean, we were in the same class with him, Harper. I watched him watching you. I watched you watching him.

HARPER

It was the most precious thing in my life; the way I adored him. It was grace. It still is.

ELAINE

You need to be in therapy Harper.

HARPER

It felt good to feel him reaching for me, dragging his hands over my ass, along my hips, resting his fingertips on my womb: the most intimate part of my body—

RYAN

Oh you're making me wet, stop it.

HARPER

I can't talk to you if you're going to be like this.

ELAINE

We should all just let each other be.

RYAN

We're a family of meddlers. Passive-aggressive meddlers. There's no possibility of 'letting be.'

HARPER

If that's true Ryan, than how do you manage to keep your business a secret from everyone else?

RYAN

Because I don't have any business to keep secret.

HARPER

Yeah right—

RYAN

I don't.

HARPER

Liar.

RYAN

No, I'm not like the rest of you—honestly—

HARPER

What does that mean?

RYAN

Uh, that I don't have super-dramatic secrets
contaminating my soul. I have a boyfriend at
school and he's nice. Big deal. You don't have to
hire a private detective like Mom did with Dad
to find that out.

HARPER laughs.

ELAINE

Ryan—how do you know about that?

RYAN

Ya'll should really learn to log out of your emails
and that 'trash' does not mean 'delete.'

ELAINE

Harper, did you know about this too?

HARPER

No: but it's funny—

ELAINE

I'm mortified. I'm so mortified.

HARPER

It is, like, pretty horrible.

RYAN

She was right though: Dad was banging someone
else—

ELAINE

The ends don't justify the means, it's something I'm ashamed of Ryan—

RYAN

Don't be though. It's just kind of funny that Dad was sleeping with his student while Harper was sleeping with her teacher—

HARPER

ASSHOLE!

RYAN

I mean, it's just really funny—

HARPER

I want to die.

RYAN

Chill the fuck out—

HARPER

No!

ELAINE

You're making you're sister uncomfortable Ryan—

HARPER

I'm not uncomfortable, I'm in pain.

ELAINE

Harper, what's wrong?

HARPER

I'm not going to explain—

ELAINE

Just tell us what you're thinking about.

HARPER

Mason.

ELAINE

Why?

HARPER

Because that's just what I do.

ELAINE

Honey, you need to think about yourself. You shouldn't be so attached to someone at this age.

HARPER

What does age have to do with what I feel?

ELAINE

It's just not a good idea...

HARPER

Why don't you want to know what he means to me? Why is everyone in such a rush to judgement?

ELAINE

I'm not you Harper, I'm just trying to understand you—

HARPER

There's no such thing as 'trying.' There's just understanding or misunderstanding. Insight or blindness.

ELAINE

Well then I guess I'm blind.

HARPER

Yes, you are.

RYAN

Am I blind?

HARPER

No: but you're an asshole, so it doesn't matter.

RYAN

I haven't see you like this since the week Pop-Pop died.

HARPER

I've always been like this!—it's always there—it just percolates—

ELAINE

You should see a therapist this week.

HARPER

I don't want to fucking see a therapist.

RYAN

What would a therapist tell her anyway Mom? Probably just to get a new family.

ELAINE

She needs someone to talk to.

RYAN

Yeah, only because the people in her life are too self-absorbed to actually listen to her.

ELAINE

Ryan, what are you accusing me of?

RYAN

Dereliction of duty.

ELAINE

Of what duty?

RYAN

The duty to have more wisdom than your children.

ELAINE

I'm going to cry.

RYAN

Go ahead. Cry. Meanwhile Harper will sit here tending to her own private universe of pain.

ELAINE

Why don't you try talking to her Ryan? Like really, sincerely, talking to her.

HARPER

I don't want ass-face to talk to me anymore.

ELAINE

Ryan, you're her best friend; just try to be kind.

RYAN

Ok, I'll try, but I can't promise anything; you
know better than I do that Poppet here is prone
to spontaneous physical and verbal lash-outs.
So, Mom, if I don't, God forbid, return with
my life, I'd like to be buried at sea by as many
handsome sailors as you can find. If you can't
find handsome sailors, make sure they're at least
muscular. That'll be fine. Muscular is fine. I'm
ok with settling. Anyway, here goes:

RYAN takes a deep breath.

RYAN

Heyyyyy Harp. Harpy. Harper. Hey buddy.
Hey sis. Hey twin. Do you wanna talk about
your Mason-induced vertigo real quick?

HARPER

Shut the fuck up.

RYAN

See.

ELAINE

Harper, I don't know what to do with you...

HARPER

Why don't you try not doing anything.

ELAINE

I'm your mother.

HARPER

Sometimes I wish you weren't.

ELAINE

I can't believe either of you.

RYAN

I know it's hard to absorb some of the hate usuaully reserved for Dad. But don't worry, he'll back soon enough.

ELAINE

I love both of you so much—

HARPER

I love you too Mom.

ELAINE

Oh Harper, I just want you to be happy.

HARPER

I want to be happy too.

RYAN

Oh God, I guess the flight from reality is about to take off. We're going to get hit with crazy baggage fees.

ELAINE

You have to let Harper and I talk the way we talk.

HARPER

Can you just go away Ryan?

RYAN

Only if you stop acting like a helpless ten year-
old.

HARPER

Why are you being such a pompous ass?

RYAN

I'm trying to help you.

HARPER

Well you're not doing a very good job.

RYAN

I don't care if you hate me, but if we're gonna
talk, we should actually talk—

HARPER

And how should we actually talk? How does
'actually' talking really sound?

RYAN

We have to concentrate our attention on the
place where words begin, not where they end.

HARPER

You're punishing me because I have what you've
always wanted: which is a fuckable cunt—

RYAN

Dost thou know the difference, my boy, between
a bitter fool and a sweet fool?

HARPER

Please, Ryan, I'm not trying to keep up with
you—

RYAN

See, there's only one way to perform
Shakespeare's plays; there's only one way to get
those colossal structures of thought airborne:
with speed and inwardness. With the violence
that comes with thinking outloud.

HARPER

Just because you learned to take it in the ass
Ryan—doesn't mean—

ELAINE

Harper—

RYAN

Doesn't mean what?

HARPER

That liberation is that easy for the rest of us.

RYAN

You're more like Dad than you realize.

HARPER

I'm tired of everybody's theories about me. No
one has any practice at what I experience on a
day-to-day basis.

ELAINE

Which is what?

HARPER

I'm not gonna say it in front of Ryan.

ELAINE

Please tell me—

HARPER

Sacred love.

RYAN

Oh! Fanastic!

HARPER

See, he's just laughing at me.

RYAN

I'm not laughing.

HARPER

Then what do you call that squealing sound?

RYAN

Recognition.

HARPER

Oh.

ELAINE
It worries me to hear you talk about your feelings for Mason like that.

RYAN
Mom, I need you to know, as clearly as possible, that you are incapable of ever saying the right thing at the right time—

ELAINE
Let Harper speak for herself.

HARPER
I think I'm done with the whole speaking thing.

ELAINE
Just tell me: should I be worried about you?

HARPER
Almost certainly.

ELAINE
I'm going to make an appointment—

HARPER
I'm drowning in place—

ELAINE
Honey—

HARPER
Don't touch me.

ELAINE
I feel bad for you.

HARPER

I'm sick of people feeling bad for me.

ELAINE

First love is always the most painful—

H ARPER

I hate it. It's fucking inhuman.

RYAN

That's probably because you're fucking someone who's inhuman.

HARPER

You know that's not true.

RYAN

Mason's a great brain that wishes it was a great heart.

HARPER

You remind me of him sometimes.

RYAN

I'm incredibly flattered, actually.

ELAINE

I think both of you need to cool it with the obsession you seem to have with this man—

HARPER

Mom—

ELAINE

I feel like it's beginning to go too far—

HARPER

I thought I had the right to live the way I wanted
to live; love the person I wanted to love. I
thought I had the right to respect; to privacy. But
I don't. I clearly don't. I have the right to act like
a neurotic, priviledged bitch or to just be nothing
at all.

RYAN

I think I heard the car—

*PAUL and MASON can be heard walking up to
the house.*

Exit HARPER, running.

*Enter MASON first, stage-center, followed by
PAUL.*

MASON goes to a window and opens it.

MASON

My grandfather used to get up in the morning
and pray, but before praying he would open the
windows. He said to me, 'There should not be
a barrier between us and God. If the windows
are closed and the shutters are closed you cannot
speak directly to God.'

RYAN

My hero.

ELAINE walks over to the window and shuts it.

ELAINE
   (to MASON)
Don't you think it's a bit cold to be opening windows?

ELAINE
   (To PAUL)
Is everything ok?

PAUL
I don't know what to tell you.

MASON
Because, you know, God is everywhere. He's in the human heart. He's in the plants. He's in the animals. He's everywhere.

ELAINE
Why is this happening?

MASON
So you have to be very careful when you speak to human beings because the man who is standing in front of you might have something divine in him.

PAUL
He's been talking like this for an hour.

RYAN

He's got some important things on his mind,
obviously—

MASON

That's right, I do—

PAUL

Oh don't provoke him—

MASON

Has anyone looked outside? There's an ocean
floating inside of nothing—

PAUL

How am I supposed to reason with a lunatic?

RYAN

By reasoning the way a lunatic would.

MASON

Not a lunatic, a dreamer—

PAUL

Oh gimme a break—

MASON

The answer to your question is: her love was a
kind of devotion.

ELAINE

We didn't ask you any questions yet—

MASON

You will. Or you won't. But that's the answer—
not to be too obvious.

RYAN

That seems obvious enough to me.

ELAINE

Paul—what did you talk about in the car?

PAUL

Ask him.

ELAINE

I'm afraid to—

MASON

There were long stretches where neither of us
spoke. Neither Paul nor I. We watched the same
houses go by and go by and by. I thought about
how, when someone dies, the clothes they leave
behind are so sad. I thought about my brother
then, naturally, and how it felt going through
his drawers after he died; how terrible it was,
not only but because we shared a room but
because I looked up to him in ways which I'd
never expressed to him.... This made me cry a
little bit. Eventually I started to talk, either to
forget how cold the car was, because Paul refused
to turn on the heat, or just because I started to
realize that there were things I wanted to say....
Alot of things.... The past just accumulates. It's
weird. People spend most of their lives wishing
the accumulated past would disappear, but it
never does. Which is why I'm here and why
everyone's freaking out. Because the past is
still there. The lived past. The living past. The
past that beats at the heart of every moment....
I always ask myself: how do you survive the
brokenness in yourself and in the world? Because
disappointment isn't a choice, it's an experience.
And yeah, I guess this is what I was talking about
it. And yeah, maybe it sounded crazy; the way I
said it. But it doesn't matter. It can't matter. It's

not supposed to matter. All I know is that for the first time in my life, I'm not afraid. All I know is that I wasn't afraid while I was waiting outside, or sitting next to Paul as we looped around the block for no reason other than to give him, and to give the rest of you, time to let one simple fact sink in. The fact, I mean, that you've only loved someone once you've glimpsed that part of them which is too beautiful to die.

ELAINE
Paul—have you gone mute?

PAUL
What do you want me to say Elaine? I'm angry at just about everyone except for Harper—

RYAN
What did I do?

ELAINE
Yeah Paul, what did Ryan do?

PAUL
Ok, let me rephrase, I'm angry at the other grown-ups in the house.

MASON
Everyone in the house is a grown-up.

PAUL
Not to me.

MASON

Age is subjective, after all.

ELAINE

(to MASON)

Do you really think that's an appropriate thing to say right now?

MASON

I wouldn't know what's appropriate—

PAUL

Obviously—

MASON

You think that's obvious?

ELAINE

Well you've been using our daughter for sex for the past four—

MASON

Excuse me?

PAUL

You heard her—

RYAN

Maybe Harper was using him for sex—

PAUL

Maybe that's what you would do Ryan—

ELAINE

Paul!

RYAN

Dad's a homophobe, I'm over it.

PAUL

I'm not a homophobe Ryan—

RYAN

Then what are you?

PAUL

It's just that when it's my own son—

ELAINE

(to PAUL)

Don't finish that sentence.

RYAN

No—let him—

PAUL

I'm going to shut up.

MASON

Maybe someone should check on Harper—

ELAINE

Don't you dare—

MASON

I didn't say that I—

PAUL

She doesn't want to be involved in this, obviously—

RYAN

What exactly is 'this'—

ELAINE

I don't know.

RYAN

Because it seems to me that what 'this' is, is an
attempt at public shaming.

ELAINE

Ryan, I would be thrilled, if anyone in this room
was something other than completely impervious
to shame—because that's the only thing anyone
should be feeling right now; for a variety of
reasons. We should be sitting with our heads
bowed.

RYAN

Ok, I have to ask again, what did I do? Why am I
a part of this pity party? I one-hundred percent
do not get it—

PAUL

This is the problem you have Ryan: you don't ever
say something nice to make someone feel better;
you insist on making sure everyone feels as bad
about themselves as possible; it's like you can't
allow yourself to empathize with what the rest of
us for one goddamn second—

RYAN

Empathize? You want me to... empathize? With you? Dad? Really? With you and Mom? With Harper? No no no no no: that's what I've strived my whole life not to do; you're right. And that distance, that *healthy* distance, is only reason I can still crack a smile while the rest of you try to think of which prescription meds you haven't tried to numb yourselves with yet. No no no no no. This is where I draw a line: associating myself, implicating myself, with everyone else's grievances against life. I've got my own, thank god, and I can't afford to borrow yours or anyone else's—

ELAINE

Oh, I'm sorry Ryan. I can't imagine how we make you feel—

RYAN

Oh, more guilt is not what's needed right now—

PAUL

Aren't we getting away from this issue at hand?

RYAN

Your smoldering, mindless rage?

MASON

Is anyone going to ask Harper what she thinks about any this conversation?

PAUL

It's not up to her to judge whether the decisions
she's made have been good ones.

ELAINE

Right—because you're the only one who gets the
judge things Paul—the father—

PAUL

Harper has always trusted me; that's all—I could
have been a resource for her; I mean, I can still be
a resource—

RYAN

I think we need to recognize that we're talking
about someone who doesn't want to be talked
about; fundamentally—

MASON

That's right—

PAUL

I would prefer it if you ceased all commentary in
regards to my daughter.

MASON

Yet, there's this order at the center of words that
commands me: speak.

ELAINE

I want to get out of here—out of this room—I'm
going to go to my room—

*ELAINE tries to exit stage-right but PAUL blocks
her way.*

PAUL

    (to ELAINE)

Don't leave me out here, right now—

ELAINE

Paul, I need to not be in this room.

RYAN

    (to MASON)

They're afraid of you.

MASON

I've noticed.

RYAN

Mom, why don't we try to negociate a resolution
here—and then everyone can take their separate
cars and go home and I'll stay here with Harper?

ELAINE

What resolution Ryan? What do you envision?

RYAN

I dunno. You propose to Mason that he assume
the role of scapegoat for the disintegration of
our family... and Mason, being a truly wise man,
accepts his scape-goating with good-natured
indifference and drives home in a state of mind
that reflects the difficult lesson he's learned about
seducing teenage girls. Dad then talks to Harper
and convinces her to once and for stop being a
vulnerable sixteen year old. Then Mom, you and
Dad amicably resolve your marital differences and
agree to be loving friends. Then, and this is the
best and most important part, I become straight,
fall in love, get married, and breed the next
generation of total maniacs. The end.

PAUL

I'm not amused.

RYAN

Hey, do you remember that year—when I was like 15 or so—when I was crying all the time and you guys forced me to go therapy? It all turned out to be amazingly simple: I admitted to the therapist—I forget her name—that I realized that I was gay because of my vague attraction to my father and then I felt fine. All I had to say was that I liked the smell of Dad's after-shave and the memory of his arms on my shoulders when he picked me up as a boy and yup! I was fine: I could move on: I knew what I was; I knew what wires were crossed up; and what I had to accept et cetera. But my theory is that somehow Dad knew that—subliminally, magically, somehow—and blamed himself: because, generally, the fact that he's so handsome makes it very difficult for him to be as boring as he wants to be, ideally—

ELAINE

I almost appreciate your humor Ryan, but it's upsetting your father.

RYAN

I don't give a shit about Dad.

ELAINE

Ryan...

RYAN

Dad, do you care what I think about you?

PAUL

I've... I've got more important things on my
mind right now; honestly.

RYAN

See Mom, he's got more important things on his
mind. There's no problem at all.

ELAINE

I don't know why I bother to try to reconcile
everyone with everyone. It's just not possible.

MASON

If no one has any questions or comments for me,
I'm going to go...

PAUL

    (to MASON)

I read your book, by the way—I didn't like it.

ELAINE

Not now Paul...

MASON

What did you hate the most about it?

PAUL

None of it made any sense—it was pretentious
beyond belief—which is what the reviews said
too—which is why you had to keep teaching
high-school; why you needed to seduce a young
girl to restore a sense of propriety to your ego—

MASON

We're both makers of beautiful, misunderstood
things, aren't we Paul? I make books and you
make Harpers.

PAUL

I don't want to hear you use her name.

MASON

I went for a walk before Harper woke up this
morning. The stars were still out, humming
above the waste of the sea. I felt, very acutely,
how devastated my inner life was; and then I
came back inside and fucked her until we both
start crying—

RYAN

Aren't you gonna say something reactionary
Dad?

PAUL

Not at the moment.

MASON

Art makes life, makes interest, makes
importance. There's no substitute for the force
and beauty of its process.

ELAINE

I think I'm having a panic attack.

RYAN

That's what you have a prescription for—

ELAINE

I need to sit down...

PAUL guides ELAINE to the couch.

ELAINE

I feel sick to my stomach—really—I feel like I'm
going to throw up.

RYAN

This is wonderful—

PAUL

It's a catastrophe—

RYAN

Why does everyone get so anxious? I feel like
nobody wants to stop and think; there's just:
action and reaction, action and reaction.

MASON

Her face is all white—

PAUL

Ryan, get your mother some water—

*RYAN goes and gets water from the
kitchenette sink.*

*He returns with the water and hands it to
PAUL, who holds it to ELAINE'S lips.*

ELAINE takes a sip and straightens up.

ELAINE

I'm fine, I'm fine. Just let go of me.

RYAN

Do you know Mom hired a private detective because she was suspicious of you? That's how she found out about you and Dizzy Lizzy—

PAUL

What?

ELAINE

Ryan...

RYAN

We were talking about it before you got here. I've known for a while—but I dunno: today seems like the day for the divesting of secrets...

PAUL shakes his head, speechless.

ELAINE

I can't believe you'd bring that up now...What's wrong with you Ryan? What's wrong with everyone?

RYAN

We have nothing better to do then try to inflict pain. It's my favorite family tradition.

ELAINE

You're my son—

RYAN

He's your husband.

PAUL

And what's Mason?—he's nothing—

MASON

That's true.

RYAN

He's the man Harper loves, for one thing.

PAUL

It's a trick on his part—

RYAN

No, Dad—it's not a trick.

PAUL

How can it not be a trick? She has no experience with men—

RYAN

Yes she does—that's the point. She has years of experience, you just don't want to hear about it.

ELAINE

That's true Paul.

PAUL

What kind of experience are we talking about
here? The experience of being treated like a toy?
The experience of having someone in a position of
authority use that authority to—

RYAN

Dad, you are not one to talk. Plain and simple.

PAUL

Fuck.

MASON

When my wife left me, I would go for long walks
every night; a hundred blocks; sometimes more.
After I met Harper, I stopped going for those
walks.

PAUL

Why are you still here?

MASON

Because our stories only carry us far enough to
see where we really need to go.

RYAN

Focus on me for a second Dad: you've got to
accept that what happened with Mason and
Harper really happened; or you risk isolating
her in a really dangerous way—

ELAINE

He's right Paul.

PAUL

No, he just lacks the maturity to understand
what's really going on here; he really does—

RYAN

I'm trying to say that Harper's tragically alone
right now, you fucking idiot—

ELAINE

Can we not raise our voices, please?

MASON

Tragedy reverses the process of causation. It
returns us to the freedom that will destroy us.

PAUL

Fucking Christ—will you stop talking nonsense?

ELAINE

It's not nonsense, actually.

PAUL

Weren't you having a panic attack a minute ago?

ELAINE

I'm fine. Someone should check on Harper. I
can't imagine how this is making her feel.

RYAN

I'll go—

Exit RYAN stage-left.

PAUL moves to exit.

ELAINE
Where are you going?

PAUL
I'm going to lay down on the bed for a second.

Exit PAUL.

ELAINE
You must think we're horrible.

MASON
I think you all suffer from being unwanted—

Enter RYAN.

RYAN
Harper's not there—

ELAINE
Oh my god.

RYAN
Her window's open—she left a note—

Enter PAUL, running.

PAUL
What happened!?

ELAINE
  Ryan what does the note say?

MASON
  It says that she's drowning.

RYAN
  That's right—that's what it says.

  Curtain.